Michael O'Loughlin was born in Dublin in 1958 and studied at Trinity College Dublin. He has published five collections of poetry, including *Another Nation: New and Selected Poems (1996)* and *In This Life* (2011). He has published numerous translations, critical essays and reviews, as well as writing screenplays and journalism. His poems have been widely anthologised and translated.

He has been Writer in Residence in Galway City and County, and Writer Fellow at Trinity College Dublin. From 1980 to 2002 he lived in Barcelona and Amsterdam, and now lives in Dublin with his wife, the singer and writer Judith Mok. He is a member of Aosdána, the affiliation of artists in Ireland.

## Praise for Michael O'Loughlin

'O'Loughlin's work is the real deal, somehow coming honestly out of and transcending its context, to straddle the line between clear-eyed honest utterance and starry-eyed word lust. What O'Loughlin publishes is slow poetry and it's worth the wait to be privy to such stilly depths. *In This Life* is wonderful.'

*Ailbhe Darcy*

'*In This Life*, therefore, is a string of jewels, dropped somewhere between Killiney and Foley Street by our wanderer in far-away lands. Carrying precious stones back from the desert, O'Loughlin reminds us yet again, that exile like death will always be part of the human condition. We are enriched for having these witness documents of his sea-faring and night-flying.'

*Thomas McCarthy*

'Here, O'Loughlin reveals a tenderness that tempers his engagement with history at the same as it enhances his portrayals of the mundane.'

*Philip Coleman*

# Poems
# 1980–2015

# Poems
# 1980–2015

## Michael O'Loughlin

NEW ISLAND

Poems 1980–2015
First published in 2017 by
New Island Books
16 Priory Office Park
Stillorgan
Co. Dublin
Ireland

www.newisland.ie

Print ISBN: 978-1-84840-543-1
Epub ISBN: 978-1-84840-544-8
Mobi ISBN: 978-1-84840-545-5

Typeset by JVR Creative India
Cover Design by Mariel Deegan
Printed by Sprint Print

New Island received financial assistance from The Arts Council (*An Chomhairle
Ealaíon*), 70 Merrion Square, Dublin 2, Ireland.

10 9 8 7 6 5 4 3 2 1

# Contents

From *The Diary Of A Silence* (1985)

From *Another Nation: New and Selected Poems* (1996)

## From *In This Life* (2011)

## Eight Poems by Mikelis Norgelis

*For Judith and Saar*

# From
## *Stalingrad: The Street Dictionary*
## (1980)

'Every tradition forbids the asking of certain
questions about what has really happened to you.'

*John Berger*

# The City

after Cavafy

You say you will leave this place
And take yourself off to God-knows-where
A Galway cottage, a village in Greece
– Anywhere but here:
Paris, Alexandria, Finglas,
The grey eroding suburb
Where you squandered the coin of your youth.
You wander down to the carriageway
And watch the lorries speeding by.
Swooning in their slipstreams
You raise your eyes in a tropical dream
To the aeroplanes overhead.

But too late you realize
That you shall never leave here!
This, or next, or any other year.
You shall pass your life, grow old
In the same suburban lounge bars
Draining the dregs of local beers
Fingering a coin in your otherwise empty pockets.
And no matter how you toss it
It always turns up the same:
The plastic sun of Finglas
Squatting on every horizon.
The squandered coin of your youth!
The slot machines you fed have rung up blanks
Not just here, but everywhere.

# The Irish Lesson

*I thank the goodness and the grace*
*That on my birth have smiled,*
*And made me in these Christian times*
*A happy English child.*

All I cared about was words
but I wouldn't learn their language;
they forced it down my five-year-old throat
I spat it back in their faces

I didn't want to learn their language
it wasn't mine

When I got too old to fear them
they appealed to a baser emotion;
I was cutting myself off
from a part of the nation's heritage

But I didn't want to know their nation's heritage
it wasn't mine

'But Mr. O'Loughlin, you're not being fair
to yourself, you know you can do better
than this. And don't forget
you'll need it for the Civil Service.'

But I didn't want to join the Civil Service

I still don't

# The Hungry Grass

This heart rotted in its pale green juice
Sickly and pale as the hungry grass
On the face of a famine grave;
But even this wasteground dreamt
Of the loving surge of cement
Against its crumbling thighs.
And then the miracle came;
The buildings shot up like gleaming teeth
Through the rotten gums of greenery
And love began to fester
Beneath the arc-lights and the jets.
Your back was cold against the ground
But your breasts were warm in my hands.
I was looking down the carriageway
And my eyes were a string of lights
Streaming into the darkness
And I thought: only this love, this city, is new.

But only one morning came
Whole in the early sun.
The concrete cracked: the sun burst grey
The buildings began to slide.
The walls collapsed
And crushed the infants in their prams.
Where were the smiling pink children?
They erupted out of the falling houses
Little bastards with eyes like stones.
They ripped out the telephone wires
And left me screaming at nobody
Standing deaf in an empty shell.
I turned the corner into their midst

And their chains reached out
And smashed my eyes and left me blind
Stumbling through these broken streets,
This ancient ground, the corpse of love
With my hands aching for somebody's throat.

# Instamatic Deaths

*A chemist's shop was broken into:*
*their bodies were found that night*
*in a basement beneath the flats*

What are they now?

I once saw a picture from Hiroshima
of a wall at the foot of a building
and you could see the people's shadows
burnt right into the stone
photographed onto the pavement
in the postures they held when exposed
to the bomb's strange artistry

Some people's lives are negatives
of photographs never developed
and some lives twist and shrivel
like strips of plastic
exposed to a flame
when a drop of chemical explodes
in a photographer's darkroom tray

On a pathway beneath the flats
I found a burnt-out flashbulb
like a bird's crushed skull
and I thought of lives now scattered
about the streets and alleys
discarded and forgotten
like faulty colour prints

The bodies lying in the basement
worn-out and blown
like cheap plastic cameras

# Medium

brrr    bright

*What?  It was the day-time?*

nnn    night    night

*Ah, it was night in the city, lit up by the bright glare of street lights.*

rrrr    wanderr

*You were wandering through the urban night.*

lone    oh    lonely

*Yes, you were lonely in the empty streets.*

oh    fair    beauty

*It was a beautiful night?*

fairvan    van    woman

*A beautiful girl, you met a beautiful girl in your wanderings. Where? Was it down by the bus stop? Beside the Chinese takeaway?*

rrr you Venus Helen of rr

*Who? Are you asking her her name?*

kot kot lin hoo lin

*No, I don't understand.*

ERNNN ERNN ERRinnn

*Erinn? Eire is the official name of the Republic of Ireland. It is written on my passport. Is that what you mean?*

aa muse coal dance plenty

*You mean some kind of forgotten harmony, some kind of Zion or Garden of Eden, and this girl reminds you of it. Is that it? You are not talking of Ireland.*

gone agone sun black broke

*This woman is gone, she has left you.*
*Why? And what is broken?*

foreign LL devil aaa

*Someone has taken this woman away from you, something terrible has happened.*

3's    3's    3's    no

*Ah yes, there are no trees, the forests are all gone. There is only the city now.*

*What? I can't hear you. You're growing faint. Try and make it louder. Try.*

gone no song music no end

*Yes.*

THE SONG IS ENDED
THE  MUSIC IS BROKEN

# Cuchulainn

If I lived in this place for a thousand years
I could never construe you, Cuchulainn.
Your name is a fossil, a petrified tree
Your name means less than nothing.
Less than Librium, or Burton's Biscuits
Or Phoenix Audio-Visual Systems –
I have never heard it whispered
By the wind in the telegraph wires
Or seen it scrawled on the wall
At the back of the children's playground.
Your name means less than nothing
To the housewife adrift in the Shopping Centre
At eleven-fifteen on a Tuesday morning
With the wind blowing fragments of concrete
Into eyes already battered and bruised
By four tightening walls
In a flat in a tower block
Named after an Irish Patriot
Who died with your name on his lips.

But watching TV the other night
I began to construe you, Cuchulainn;
You came on like some corny revenant
In a black-and-white made for TV
American Sci-Fi serial.
An obvious Martian in human disguise
You stomped about in big boots
With a face perpetually puzzled and strained
And your deep voice booms full of capital letters:
What Is This Thing You Earthlings Speak Of

# Mandelstam

A woman's voice full of fear and pain
Dragged me awake
From my sleep's dark honey,
Blinking in the dark apartment
Like a flaccid wasp
Or something from Kafka.
I lay without moving.
And then the rattle and bark
Of her steel-tongued interrogator.
Plausible terror,
Uniformed chaos.
I got up and opened the door
And looked down the flood-lit corridor;
A man and woman stood there
Talking and laughing
Like natural lovers.
They never even glanced at me.
I went back inside
Lay down on my bed
Tried to sleep but couldn't
With a needle stuck in my heart:
*I heard what I heard*
*I heard what I heard*

# The Journey

for days the hum of rubber and oil
the screaming whisper of trucks
as they passed; we followed
a grey rainbow through
faceless green countryside
kicked our heels in parking lots
a sentimental distance
from the road; drank coffee
in motorway stations clean
and familiar as a Hamburg whore
2 AM, 7 KMS from the blue sign
for a cathedral town
slumbering in red brick
we watched a flickering TV set
with the sound switched off
behind us we heard the ignition click
of spoon in coffee cup;
two men, commercial travellers we thought
they followed us out to where
the road was picking up speed
we drove off calm, wondering
down a stairway into the dark
while the night filled with static
and a song in another language
we sat flattened to our seats
while the night broke its limits
and the rectangle of our headlamps
became a square, and then
for a fraction of a second
a white line shooting
into the dead star
at the heart of things

# Yellow

I stamped through the pastures
booting the heads off buttercups
I stormed in out of the wheatfield
into a country kitchen
and let out my gurrier roar:
'Yellah! Yellah! Yellah!'
But she took me on her knee
and said: no, it's yellow.
I glowed, I echoed yellow
but that was a colour
I had never seen
till I saw her stretched on a hospital bed
the yellow of cancer and nicotine

# Babel

She is a language I will never speak
– great is my sorrow this night.
I will never whiten a wall for her
nor make the grass grow greener.
Her skin was the colour of honey
stored by the bees in the damp river bank
– where the sun himself had not kissed her
it was cream in a cool stone kitchen
in the stillness of a summer's day.

In the purple dusk by the walled-in river
she glowed as she stood in the street.
I had never seen such a sight before
and even the traffic parted that she might pass.
Great was the sorrow I could not speak
in the room where we sat that night
– as a man who stands upon a hill
in a place of ancient renown
and hears a phrase of a song
float up from the valley below
like a wisp of white smoke
from a sacred fire
that burns in the sun at noon
– and he knows not what it speaks of
nor learning nor lonesome quest
through dusty book and library
shall be of any use to him.
Blessed is he who is her song!
Blessed with her skin of honey and cream
her perfect instep of soft kid's leather
and thigh like a pillar wrought
by some miraculous Greek.

Blessed is he, and cursed am I
with nothing to keep me from madness and death
but this dull unlovely translation!

# Copenhagen Dreaming Of Leningrad

Warszava, the plaintive flute of the East,
Its ancient wooden melody bent
To the cello and drums of Moscow.

Over the drunken green Baltic
A black wind full of snow
Carries the straining orchestra.

Like the sand shifting beneath the waves,
Like the slash of flesh on bone!
Warszava, Warszava, I am drunk with your name

Till the glass-green Baltic floods
Like the mind of a mad composer
With the wind's unplayable melody

And the mountains scale the ground
To a symphony's frozen climax!
The note is held and then begins

The slow bass beat of Stadt and Grad
– A shimmer, and water is frozen:
Seductive and brutal as massed violins
The choral cathedral of Lenin!

# From
*Atlantic Blues*
(1982)

# The Front Line

I

Neat khaki, helmets
covering most of their faces
and like a luminous nail
in a crucifix, a yellow silk scarf
carefully knotted
about the throat.
Casually dangling machine-guns
they stand about,
dressed to kill.

II

Down behind the cathedral
a girl was selling mechanical doves.
You wound them up
and flung them into the air
and they flew, rattling,
gracelessly
flapping mechanical wings.
The pigeons that scuffle
about the crowd
scattered in terror
as it flew towards them.
With cold sweating eyes
they watched it from their boltholes
up in the cathedral roof.

III

That was how the people scattered
on Thursday night
at the top of the Ramblas
when they charged
with batons drawn.
One of them crossed my path
like a runaway tank, all jangling metal
and awful momentum.
I bolted into a café
and watched the rows of riot police
forming up outside.

IV

Later,
I walked home down the gauntlet,
a living wall
of khaki, steel, and silk.
Although I wasn't lost I asked one for directions.
He was friendly and courteous
and drew me a map
on a page torn from his notebook.
Leaning forward
to explain some point
the rim of his cold steel helmet
touched my sweating forehead.

# *From* Limerick, 1919

III

What fascinates me are the possibilities
Present in every event
The actors reading their lines
Not knowing how the script will end.
The say the winners write the history books
And history's pen moved plausibly enough
Across the pages of Nineteen Nineteen
The phrases and slogans ringing out
Like the eventual victor's artillery
The long periods plausible
Leading up to the present full stop –
The national anthem blaring out
After the evening's TV viewing
From which I retrace my steps.
But time clicks on with its square eyes open –
And all their lies are in vain
As I found when I went to rummage
Through the discarded footage of history
And found that this was our pathetic Petrograd
Nestling like some virgin Aztec city
In the hidden valleys of history
Lost to the Conquistadore's maps.
What a film it would have made
For some home-grown Eisenstein!
But it was not to be.
We walk out into the flat Dublin evening
Full of uncertain nostalgia
For a past we didn't have
After watching Bertolucci's *Novocento*
Authentic but slightly stagy

Like a young Russian poet
Praising Lenin and airports.
But what does it matter
That we have no films, no flags
No carefully annotated traditions.
History cannot be stolen, only hidden;
It still lives on
In the unpurgeable underground of the blood
And as for us, our history has barely begun.
All over Ireland
The suburbs are swelling with children
Like a river of liquid concrete
Drowning the old monuments
And all around us, secretly, invisibly
The air is crackling with Radio Dublin
And soon the sleeping suburbs will wake
To the ragged secret chorus
Of alarm clocks going off
And people will march in their thousands
Down the stairs in the still black
Winter morning
And lights spring on in the window of every kitchen
Lighting up all over, the humble constellations.

# Venus In Concrete

I'm standing at the bus stop at the shopping centre
Facing the camera, slightly right of,
The background is the concrete wall
That runs down to the Bank of Ireland
Behind me the Venus de Milo
Grows out of the bricks at a crazy angle
The passers-by don't even notice
And then I realise it's not on camera
It's a portrait I've painted of myself
And then I know it's a dream
But I've never awoken out of this dream
Merely embellished, allowed it to seep
Through my life, smoothing it out like acrylic
And the dream flowed into words
Lifting them off the page
Like people stepping out of a TV screen
And Heaven, what was Heaven for example?
It was a cool gallery, modern and white
With powerful lighting and a glossy catalogue
And a girl attendant who was something I can't remember
And I can't remember, barely able
To distinguish the fantasy from the dream
The dream from mutating reality
And it's like the evening in Finglas
When everything's quiet
The incomprehensible mountains
Visible over Finglas South
And the concrete strains against the dusk
And it's like reading a bad translation
Of a poem by a great Czechoslovakian poet...
Like ice in the river, that's what we're like

That's what I tell myself day after day
Standing in the Metro on my way to work
Walking from bar to bar –
Like ice in the river, that's what I say
What does it matter, the drip
Of the sailor's tears in the ocean?
And I think of the image and what it's worth
And realise that even here
Obscurity is sometimes acceptable
Like Natasha and Sonia in *War and Peace*
Who never mentioned Prince Andrei
Because his memory was too sacred
And one day found they'd forgotten him
I no longer know which is the truth
And which is the dream
Except what I need
And I need to believe that this is me
Walking the streets
Pacing the walls of the English language
Looking for a chink in the concrete
That will let in my own light...

# Hamlet In Dublin

The trains have stopped running
The theatres are closed
My shoulders are bruised
From the narrow corridors
That lead out onto the stage

I rehearse all night in the bars
I stagger and fall, declaiming
And Oh my friends
There is something rotten
In this State of ours

The carpark echoes with my voice
The streetlamps blaze like footlights
And out in the darkness beyond them
I suddenly realise
There's no audience

# Boxer

The days lurch towards me like a punch-drunk boxer
Swinging away with their horrible hammy fists
Pummelling away, unable to hurt me
– But I can't bring myself to avoid them,
With their battered Ernest Borgnine faces
And their cauliflower ears
And their stupid swollen horse's eyes
Begging me to let them win

I can't bring myself to look at you
My head squats down on my chest
Like an old bag full of sawdust
And we continue, and the heart endures,
The heart in its red tent
A crushed head with a boxer's face
Its eyes clogged with blood
Blood streaming out of its ears

# End Of An Affaire

On the first day I welcomed your teeming battalions
Your iron wing clattering through the ghetto's maze
I cheered and wept as your tanks and troops
Came rolling down my tired and bloody streets

On the second day you posted your first decrees
And my wildest children were out on the street
Beseeching you with curses and stones
Cars became bombs, the streets were arsenals

On the third day came the first of my deaths
I followed the corpse to the freezing graveyard
And came back with steel in my heart

On the fourth day you came for my manhood
And dragged it away to your camp
Slowly, old patterns emerged
Obscure causes, ancient wrongs

On the fifth day our politicians met round the table
Sweating and hoarse, shouting
And arguing into the night
Seeking the compromise, the slow way forward

On the sixth day our Government finally collapsed
And the fighting went on all night
The iron barriers went up between us
My heart was a no-go area

The seventh day passed without incident
In a state of tensed normality
I blurted out an occasional sentence
Like an insane housewife rushing into the street

On the night of the seventh day
Darkness came, you called a curfew
Taking the gun from beneath the floorboards
Where it had lain such a long time
My heart went out to hunt you down

# The Fugitive

In the hours before the Metro opens
I remember you, Richard Kimble
With my hands dug deep in my jacket pockets
Walking the streets of a foreign city.

Tonight I suddenly remember it all –
The damp winter nights in Dublin
The living room with the curtain undrawn
And the streetlight spilling in

And myself, silent, hypnotised
Stretched out on the orange lino
Lost in the numinous images
Of the TV's black and white glow

And scarred by smoke and city dawns,
The muffled snarl of American accents
Coming in loud and razor sharp
Over the local interference.

I can't remember the stories now
But in the end it's only the ikons that matter,
The silent, anonymous, American city
With the rain running down the gutter

And the snatched glimpse of the one-armed man
Sinking back into the shadows,
The real victim, the truly guilty
The man you're destined to follow.

This life, this city fits me
Like an old leather jacket
Picked up for nothing
In a second-hand market

And I light up a cigarette
Relaxing in the casual rhyme
That floats through the city
Binding other lives to mine

And like so many times before
I turn up my collar against the wind
And walk off down the dark side of the street
Dreaming already of another town

Remembering you, Richard Kimble
And the way you taught me to live;
Ending another forgotten episode
Still myself, still The Fugitive.

# Two Women

*Nadezhda Mandelstam*

In the damp brown evening of early winter
I see him stumbling along through the frozen mud
Across the bridge at the edge of town
With nothing but the broken harp of himself
On the forced march of days
Towards a battle he'd rather avoid
With his life, his hope,
Trudging a long way behind him
His music held tight in her aching fingers.


*Lotte Lenya*

Give her a tune and she'll break it they said
And she did, just like the world that she lived in.
The boys in the leather jackets
Were hardly surprised to find her
The goddess with the nightclub sneer
And a voice like the ruins of Berlin
Because no matter what they played on the radio
Day followed day like notes
In harsh, unheard-of harmonies
Where the tune can only survive
On the black bread of love.

# After A War

Adolescence, too, is a civil war.
I sit in the park
My body purrs in the sun.
The traffic streams by full of purpose
And the shops are full of goods
And people to buy them.
I am as empty as a population
Purged of unwanted elements.
*La Guerre est finie...*
I think of nothing except my work
A beer, a smoke, a sandwich.
All I want is you,
The exotic bread of your hair
Your hand in mine,
Facing the night together.
I look at the old men sitting in the sun
With their berets and memories,
Their sticks and stumps.
Blankly, we look at each other.
*None of it had any importance*
*None of it was real*
*Or else we would have died of grief*
*Who didn't die of wounds.*

# Tibidabo

Morning stretched taut across the city
Pounded by the screaming kids in the schoolyard
Resolving their rhythms into African drums.
In laboratories all over the city
Oscilloscopes smoothly choreograph
The calm waves of immeasurable forces.
Stasis: like the two small dots of a colon
My eyes look out over stasis:
Millions of lives pulling in opposite directions
Vans full of goods are despatched to the suburbs
The presses run their black tongues
Over the paper's white belly.
Our hands recognise each other.
The sun stutters down through gaps in the buildings
The city wipes its sweat with the air.
You are the opal in the city's navel;
Millions of invisible lines sprout from your eyes
The day runs down through its scales
We shiver at the peak of millions
Of windows and car rooves flashing.
The city hangs in the light-blue smog
Like a symphony orchestra suspended over the ocean
One wrong note and the whole thing will fall
Quietly, we sit at the table, singing

# From
## *The Diary Of A Silence*
## (1985)

'...the whole world is suburb
Where are the real towns?'

*Marina Tsetaeva*

# An Irish Requiem

*i.m. Mary Lynch, 1897–1983*

Born in another country, under a different flag
She did not die before her time
Her god never ceased to speak to her.
And so she did not die. The only death that is real
Is when words change their meaning
And that is a death she never knew
Born in another country, under a different flag.
When the soldiers and armoured cars
Spilled out of the ballads and onto the screen
Filling the tiny streets, she cried
And wiped her eyes on her apron, mumbling something
About 'the Troubles'. That was a word
I had learned in my history book.
What did I care for the wails of the balding Orpheus
As he watched Eurydice burn in hell?
I was eleven years old,
And my Taoiseach wrote to me,
Born in another country, under a different flag.
She did not die before her time
But went without fuss, into the grave
She had bought and tended herself, with
The priest to say rites at her entry
And the whole family gathered,
Black suits and whiskeys, a cortège
Of Ford Avengers inching up the cemetery hill.
Death came as an expected visitor,
A policeman, or rate collector, or the tinker
Who called every spring for fresh eggs,
Announced by the season, or knocks on walls,

Bats flying in and out of rooms, to signify
She did not die before her time
Her god never ceased to speak to her.
Till the last, he murmured in her kitchen
As she knelt at the chair beside the range
Or moved to the damp, unused, parlour
For the priest's annual visit.
*Poète de sept ans*, I sat on the polished wood,
Bored by the priest's vernacular harangue
As she knelt beside me on the stone church floor,
And overheard her passionate whisper,
Oblivious, telling her beads, and I knew
That I would remember this, that
Her god never ceased to speak to her.
And so she did not die. The only death that is real
Is when words change their meaning
And that is a death she never knew.
As governments rose and fell, she never doubted
The name of the land she stood on. Nothing
But work and weather darkened the spring days
When she herded her fattened cattle
Onto the waiting cars. It is not she who haunts
But I, milking her life for historical ironies,
Knowing that more than time divides us.
But still her life burns on, like the light
From a distant, extinguished star, and
O let me die before that light goes out
Born in another country, under a different flag!

# The Shards

'In the North we are not only on the cold edge of civilization, but also on that of being, truth and life itself. Naked imaginative field...'

*Asger Jorn*

*I. The Bunkers*

Along the great coast south of Bordeaux
The bunkers still stare out to sea
High-water marks of the black wave
That swept up out of the sump of Europe.
Untouched, they stand, undying monuments,
Easter Island heads in cold concrete.
On the side of one I found
Some Gothic lettering, black paint
That hadn't faded in the years of sun and wind.
But the blonde naked daughters
Sleep rough in them during the summer nights
And in the morning run laughing
Into the ocean their fathers had scanned.

*II. The Birds*

Somewhere north of Lille
I stared at the sea of white crosses
Like sea birds resting on the earth.
So much suddenly real!

*III. Frank Ryan Dead In Dresden!*

The idea armed, like Ernie O'Malley
Another emerald-green incorruptible
Of course there was no place for the likes of you!
When you came bounding out of the prison camps
To join the shuffling battalions
Into the civil service offices
They gave you a job writing tourist brochures.
'Killarney is famous the wide world over
For the magnificent splendour
Of its mountains and lakes...'
And after, you marched off into the night
To practice the illegal alchemy
Of slogans and heavy printer's ink.
Now it speeds up. A handsome head, in uniform.
Then defeat. The tale grows complex.
Europe dividing under your feet.
Conspiracies, betrayals, and all the rest.
In that last passport photo taken in Berlin
You look like Rembrandt in his last self-portrait.
There is much there I don't know, nor want to.
You followed your river into the sea,
And drowned, while your funeral pyre
Lit up the skies for a hundred miles around.

*IV. From A Diary*

I seem to have travelled this landscape for years.
Brown hulks of deserted factories, the dark wounds
Of their shattered windows, fragments of glass
Defying the wind. The yellow blocks of flats
And behind them, the endless ordered fields
Flecked with rusted iron.
The train slowed down near a flat broad river
And I saw fields full of green machines
Stretching out into the distance,
Tensing on black rubber. A lone sentry
Stood out against the skyline, looking in no
Particular direction. Behind him a filthy grey sky
Floundered into the night.

## V. Heinrich Böll In Ireland

We slept through it. A stray bomber,
a black sheep strayed from the pack
Came crackling in out of the watching darkness.
Later, some stumbled across our shores
In search of a green poultice
For wounds we couldn't have understood.
There, at last, a small destiny, ours.
This also: the skyways criss-crossed
By peaceful jets, their passengers reading
In magazines about the
Most profitable
Industrial
Location
In Europe.

## VI. Concert-Going In Vienna

Our houses are open tombs that will survive us.
And so are our lives. No one survives a war like that.
That is obvious; also ridiculous.
Our eyes blink in the sullen gleam of the knife
But do not see the submerged balancing weight
Beneath the cutting edge. Tonight, I feel it
The solid drag, the tug and undertow
Of centuries of prosperity, watching
These faces and manners planed by music,
I had not thought death had missed so many.
This woman here in front of me, for instance
In pearls and grey hair in a stately bun
Nodding her head in time to Bruckner's Fourth.
She is not dead, nor am I. The sublime
And gracious she samples as familiar delicacies
And it is churlish of me to criticise this.
But still, I know, from the ranks of satisfied diners
A hungry ghost slips off into the forest
Trying on coats of clay for size.

## VII. The Boys Of '69

'I don't know why we didn't go –
we talked about nothing else.'
But they didn't go, didn't die
On the barricades of '69,
They survived to cushy jobs
In Luxembourg and Brussels.
Cushy but hopeless!
'Sure we hadn't a chance boy!
What do you think?
The French and the Dutch
were already dug in.'
He peels the silver wrapping
Off another bottle of beer.
I watch the alien sun sink red
Behind the blocks of flats.
'Poor Sean! They found his body
out there on the beach. Nothing
ever proved, of course. Never
saw him depressed. A boy
to drink though, he was barred
from the British Embassy
after that night,
I remember it well...'
I suddenly see him, poor Sean,
With his Aran sweater
And second-class degree in history
A pale-faced corpse
Drifting like a dead fish
Through a sea of foreign newsprint
Red-bearded idol of a scattered army
Of terylene shirts and expense accounts
In half the capital cities of Europe...

## VIII. *The Shards*

For months, coming home late at night
We would stop at a traffic light
In the middle of nowhere
And sit there, the engine restless
For the empty motorway
While I looked out at the half-built flyovers
That stood in the moonlight
Like a ruined Greek temple
And I suddenly felt surrounded
By the shattered and potent monuments
Of a civilization we have not yet discovered
The ghost of something stalking us
The future imagined past perhaps
Or else the millions of dead
Rising and falling
Into the mud and carved stone
The ghost of the beast
Whose carapace we inhabit
Not knowing if we stand
At centre or circumference
Sensing that shards are our only wholeness
Carefully carving their shattered edges.

# From A Café

'Fósforo y fósforo en la oscuridad
Lagrima y lagrima en la polvareda.'
                                    *César Vallejo*

Last night I dreamt you were in my room
In my sleep I felt your presence
Like fine rain on my nerve ends
But when I struggled awake you were gone.

You've blown through me like nuclear fallout
And left me reeling, sick in my bones
Nursing my sickness in suburban cafés
Where the coffee bubbles with faith in mankind.

Match after match in the dark
Tear after tear in the dust
The waitress brings me cup after cup
While I hide my face in a foreign tongue.

# Posthumous

Something is pushing against my blood.
From the bus I watch the children
Set fire to sheets of paper
And scatter them, screaming, into the wind.
They burn down to nothing,
A black smudge on the concrete
Bleeding its greyness into the sky.
I think of Siberia, how clean it is.
I move around the city, denounced
To the secret police of popular songs.
A name flares in the darkness.
Moon-sister, twin.
Who are you? I don't know.
My mouth tastes of splintered bone.
I thought I'd left this place a long time ago.

# The Diary Of A Silence

In Parnell Square it's always raining
On the junk heap of history where I was born
One wet night, in the Rotunda Hospital
While the crowds surged down O'Connell Street
And the shades did cluster round
My state-assisted birth, in this elephant's
Graveyard under grey skies!

The damp, disintegrating houses
Shuffle shoulder to shoulder through time
Stuffed with religious statues and creaking
Rooms, empty, forgotten, memorial halls
Marked by cracked plaques and faded signs
Of chipped gilt over fanlights
Everything living its posthumous existence
Hungering in me for an image
That is not mere archaeology
The casual coupling of history and self.

I probed the city's cracked grey ribs,
Noted the casual irony
Of the tottering Georgian tenements!
But one day they were gone
Thesis devoured by antithesis
Oratory swallowed by irony
Cancelling each other out
Leaving not even an aftertaste
Just silence tensing towards the word
That will define it,
In a language that doesn't yet exist.

Where the buildings once had stood
The sky rushed into their virgin spaces
The mad light of Dublin battering my face
The great expressionist winter sky
Where light and dark wrestle like primitive gods
Like complex chemical formulae
Something struggling to become itself.

It has always been like this. What can be said
Is not worth saying, will not still the itch
That has always possessed me, gripped
And held fast from the start
And would not release, or burst into flower
Except suddenly, laboriously,
Like turning the corner into Parnell Square
To see the yellow buses throbbing in the rain
Pristine, orphic: obmutescent.

# Two Poems For Paddy Graham

*1. Summer in Monaghan*

my mouth is daubed with black and green!
gulping mouthfuls of dark air
black flags hang from the telegraph poles
this land is a hunger
I cannot breathe
love lies like a plague on the land
love? The greyness of summer?
(who are those faces, bright
and I think, familiar,
names, old loves, stirring
like nails in their rusty sockets?)

a black sea rocks us to sleep

in the morning the darkness lightens
between the murderous drumlins
the roads are smeared
with small furred corpses
sometimes a sweet rain rinses the air
water colours a faint illusion
(in the dead hiss of a summer's evening
a lake has drifted from Persia)

## 2. *Heimat*

All over Ireland the black light falls.
On the rotting stone houses of
Provincial towns,
And on the pristine office blocks;
On the nervous green fields
And cold suburban roads.
This was home, as a child I knew it.
The black clouds soaked in radiance
Exploding softly on the Wicklow Mountains
Marching west in a dinosaur train
Across the wet slate roofs, bobbing
Heavily forward with brute momentum
And grace, leaving their footprints
In my mind, deserts hungry
For remembered weather, like your canvas hungry for paint
Each painting a difficult homecoming
A muddy thaw, savage archaeology, the slow
Decolonisation of childhood,
Letting us see
What is in the black light visible.

# The Smile

Late summer. A Dublin Sunday,
hushed and heavy
my soles scrape the pavement

There was a smell
of burning rubber
from the park behind the flats

A policeman on a motorbike
zig-zagged
the afternoon streets

A remote-control toy
smudging the air
with demon voices

A young man with a Mexican moustache
stood casual guard
as two children played in the gutter

I approached from a long way off
to ask him the way;
he answered slowly

As I watched the phoenix
sketched
on the chest of his T-shirt

'Never heard of it. But
I'll tell you this much.
It's nowhere near this kip.'

And we smiled
like the future regarding the past
or vice versa

# Three Fragments On The Theme Of Moving Around In Cities

*I. Epitaph For Matt Talbot*

'Skua!', 'Skua!', the gulls shriek
Skiting above the stinking Liffey
Where your name flaps
Like a plastic sack
Along the deserted quays
In the minds of old women
Carrying their shopping
From chapel to chapel.

*II. Little Suburban Ode*

In our cold, gloomy Napoli
Pasolini's Nordic children
Cruise the icy pot-holed streets
In stolen diplomatic limos

Rocketing round the broken corners
Like steel balls in a pinball game
Before they fly right off the board
– Or slot home safely in the suburbs.

*III. Berlin*

Under a bruised sky the empires meet
And freeze. I don't like that I like it here,
The cold stench of flesh become stone
The palled appalling innocence of the heart
A giddy dog loping through ruins
A god on the morning of creation
His mouth full of juicy bones.

# One version of a myth

I scribbled poems
in the back of
my chemistry notebook
about the survival
of primitive man
into the techno-
logical era.
But they didn't
answer my question.
At evening I always
found myself here
in one place or another
watching the dusk descend
on the shuttered suburbs
splash the skyline
with chemical red
and then
the light was gone –
suddenly swallowed
by billowing clouds
of octopus black –
tomorrow it would return
in lines
of field-grey infantry
straggling in
across the coast road
and the frozen sand
choked on the corpses
of birds
and old rubber tyres.

I stood
on this cold battlefield
choking on fear
and the February air
walked
between the silent blocks
the steel-grilled shops
the streets shuttling
endlessly
back into each other –
I felt that we were
strapped tight
hurtling towards
some moment in space and time
we could not construe
or else that this speed
was the illusion of stasis
there was no escape
no meaning
in this prison
of concrete and night
– I lit cigarettes
and smoked them
to communicate
with some
heroic spirit
remembered from my childhood
– I consoled myself
with the sound
of my steel-heeled boots
on the plates
of the railway bridge

# The East Wind

Straight from Siberia, our mothers said,
The East wind blew in off the Irish Sea
To freeze us between the rows of houses
Where we ran in the glaring yellow light
To chase a dirty white plastic ball
Skittering along the concrete.

Our faces were frozen in monkey grins,
Our hands were completely numb
And when we fell flying onto the pavement
We did not feel a thing, nor stop
To check our limbs, but struggled up
To woodenly run on, not thinking
Of the relief and pain that would come
With the thaw.

# Intensity, Exaltation

*after Vallejo*

I want to write, but I foam at the mouth
There's so much to say but I get bogged down;
There's no number uttered which isn't a sum,
No pyramid written without a green heart.

I want to write, but I sense the puma;
I ask for laurel, but they give me an onion.
There's no sound made which doesn't grow vague,
There's neither god nor son of god without development.

So come on then, let's eat grass,
Fruit of weeping, flesh of moans,
Jam made out of our melancholy souls.

Come on! Come on! I am wounded;
Let's drink what's already been turned into piss,
Come on, mister crow, let's go to your missus.

# Elegy For The Unknown Soldier

'It is hard to read on the ancient stone...
In the month of Athyr Levkios fell asleep.'
*Cavafy*

One evening in August, the light already failing
An insurance salesman dropped me off at a crossroads
In Cavan or Monaghan, the beginning of the drumlin country.
I stood there for a while, near a newly-built bungalow
Watching the green fields darken behind a screen of hedges.
Just where the roads met there was a sort of green
With a JCB parked right up on the verge
And a small celtic cross of grey granite.
I walked over to read the inscription
Peering through the fading light.
'Patrick O'Neill, Volunteer, Third Belfast Brigade
Shot on a nearby hillside. 16 April 1923.'
I can't remember exactly, but that was the gist of it.
By the time I finished reading, it was completely dark.
All the lights were on in the nearby bungalow,
I could see the TV screen through the living-room window.
I heard the engine of a car in the distance,
The cone of its headlights appearing and disappearing.
He stopped and gave me a lift to Cootehill. I didn't look back.

# The Black Piano

The language turns to mush in our mouths –
Like the brown slush flooding the streets
Beneath my window. But now it's snowing,
White flakes falling on the frozen canals.
In my room, I turn the pages of Russian books
Trying to understand, knowing
That the storm that swept them away
Is the storm that swept me here
To stand in the place where they once stood
My head ringing with their echoes.
Through the walls of my room I hear
The tuneless tentative notes
Of my neighbour's pupils,
Their fingers stumbling over the keyboard.
Coming home late at night, I like
To climb the steps and peer
Into her tiny front room,
Filled with a frozen black piano
Basted with hidden light, like a shrine.
In my room I stalk on,
Imagining listeners behind the white wall
Their ears bent to the tuneless tentative sound
Of my black boots plodding through virgin snow.

# Valparaiso

He sat in the gloom like a dim Buddha
His bald head gleaming
In the faint light filtering into the room.
There was a smell of damp earth in the hallway
The heavy long sadness of ancient forest floors
Where the sun has never shone. We entered
From the chilly marble stairs, still splashed
With light and shouts from the street outside
And stumbled over the screens and tapestries
Low sofas festooned with Indian designs
That he patiently crafted here, in the back streets
Of a tourist town.
                          He was no Indian, though silent
And patient as one, and his large brown eyes
Were like the stolen eggs of some exotic bird
That dreams of mountains and circling, circling
Through brilliant skies. The light
Assaulted the blinds that hadn't been open in years
Filtering into the room in slits
Illuming snatches of dust.
Someone whispered his story in my ear, the usual
One I'd heard before; economist
In the Allende government, flight and exile,
His wife had left him for a minor diplomat,
Leaving him with children behind.
But none of this seemed relevant to his immobile
Vegetable sadness, which raddled the air
Like a dry stain. His son put on his leather jacket
Went out to hunt *rubias* in the local discos
Up on the roof I bounced a ball
With his neurotic daughter

Her vowels already rounded by Catalan.
Later that night, Luis arrived to cook the meat.
Nervy, garrulous, Argentinian,
Cursing Spain and leaving it behind him
His tickets home already bought.
We talked about Borges and Spanish football
Our faces red with the heat of the coals
While down in the streets, the tourists drifted
Through valleys of floodlit sculptured flowers.
I woke next morning before anyone else,
And padded through the hallway. Through the open door
I saw him laid on his bed like a toppled idol,
Barely breathing, in the other bed his daughter
Restless and creased, a dark snake in the undergrowth.
The light drilled into the walls. Outside,
It was Sunday on the beach, the trains
Came lurching and rocking out of Barcelona
Searing in the heat, packed with people
Their limbs already turning brown.
Before we left that afternoon
We sat once more in the gloom to sing some songs
And he strummed a simple melancholy dance
Over and over again, on the strung shell of an armadillo,
And falling through the years,
I saw a winter's morning of fear and booming voices
My hands cold clutching the varnished wood
While I painfully glossed a Gaelic poem
About a ship sailing out of Valparaiso
And how its purple echo had sailed with me
To this strange harbour, this unmapped land,
To dance now to the Charrango!

# Anne Frank

*(What we cannot speak about,*
*We must pass over in silence...)*

Life is lived in rooms like this.
That, at least, we can say.
And people come and go
On speakable missions,
Clear commands. And we can talk
And smother the air with words
Till we feel we understand.

In these rooms we sleep and dream
And rise to breakfast on white linen.
There are books to read,
And at night the scratch
Of pen and paper.

Life is lived in rooms like this
Where we lean towards a square of light
But where the walls are
We can only discover
By walking out into that darkness
Fingers outstretched, blind
Knowing we have no words
For what we may find.

# Exiles

In all the dead ends of Dublin
you will find the Italian chippers
abandoned, forgotten consulates
of obscure Apennine villages
whose chocolate-box picture
sometimes hangs
above the bubbling friers.
Again and again
they dispense our visas
sealed with salt and vinegar
wrapped in greaseproof paper.
Somehow we never go.

The old consul
has grown sardonic.
He stares out the steamed-up
windows at the rain,
the file of bored taximen
waiting at the rank.
His eyes glint with vendetta.
He lights up another Sweet Afton

turns to glare at his sons
who have mastered the local dialect,
leaning across the counter
to chat with their friends.
Sometimes, without warning
they all begin
to shout in Italian
like Joyce and his children.

# On Hearing Michael Hartnett
# Read His Poetry In Irish

First, the irretrievable arrow of the military road
Drawing a line across all that has gone before
Its language a handful of brutal monosyllables.

By the side of the road the buildings eased up;
The sturdy syntax of castle and barracks,
The rococo flourish of a stately home,

The formal perfection and grace
Of the temples of neoclassical government
The avenues describing an elegant period. Then,

The red-brick constructions of a common coin
To be minted in local stone, and beyond them
The fluent sprawl of the demotic suburbs

Tanged with the ice of its bitter nights
Where I dreamt in the shambles of imperial iambs,
Like rows of shattered Georgian houses.

I hear our history on my tongue,
The music of what has happened!
The shanties that huddled around the manor

The kips that cursed under Christchurch Cathedral
Rising like a madrigal into the Dublin sky
– But tonight, for the first time,

I heard the sound
Of the snow falling through moonlight
Onto the empty fields.

# Latin As A Foreign Language

I suppose I should feel somehow vindicated
 To see our declensions bite deeper
  Than our legionaries' swords –
   But somehow I don't.
   We're a mixed lot here, devils
 To drink; old senatorial types and
Discarded favourites, poets without patrons etc.

When asked why they're here they might answer
 About duty to the empire, missionary zeal
  Or simply the spirit of adventure –
   All rot, of course.
   No one leaves Rome unless
 He has to, or not exactly because he has to
Like a vulgar soldier in a conscripted legion

But things somehow *conspire* to force him out.
 Not all poets find patrons, not all
  Fit smoothly into public life –
   You know how it is.
   One wrong word in the wrong ear
 One fateful opportunity fluffed, and
You may as well forget it. Who understands these things?

Some say they lie in the lap of the gods but either way
 We end up here in the backwaters of empire
  Drumming our illustrious tongue
   Into barbarian skulls
   And polishing up the phrases
 Of the oafs who govern in Rome's name.
Like I said, a mixed lot, refugees all from obscure failures.

Some marry local girls, and sprout blonde beards
   And curls overnight. Poor bastards!
     How can they take seriously
      Those bovine bodies
     Those gaudy faces lisping bad breath.
    Who could write poetry for such as these?
I think about these things a lot, but come to no conclusion.

During the freezing winter nights sitting round the wine
   And olives, telling tales of sunnier days
     Sucking ancient bits of gossip
      Down to the dry pit
     Cato elaborates his pet theory;
   How Rome will someday crumble to dust
Beneath the barbarian heel, and only our precious language

Will survive, a frail silken line flung across the years.
   But I don't know. Who among these barbarians
     Would give a fart in his bearskin
      For Horace or Virgil
     Or any of us? All they want is enough
    To haggle with a Sicilian merchant, or cheat
The Roman tax collector out of his rightful due.

But late at night, when I stumble out into
   The sleet and cold I was not born to
     And feel the threatening hug
      Of those massive forests
     Stuffed with nameless beasts
    And the great godless northern sky
Threatening me with its emptiness and indifference

To me and all that are like me – then, sometimes,
  I think he may be right; that
    We are the galley slaves
      Sweating below
    Bearing the beautiful
  Princess who sits in the prow
Across the ocean to her unknown lover.

# The Real Thing

I shuffled the musty floorboards
Of your emporium, stuffed with baubles
And useless knick-knacks, melancholy
Mechanical toys from Hong Kong, that soon
Fell asunder, scattering pieces of coloured tin
And stone-age plastic all over the house,
Like indecipherable relics.

Where did you come from? I like
To think of you, a grey-bearded shuffler
Peddling your goods all round the Baltic
From Lübeck and Lublin to Dublin
Where the pale children from the nameless suburbs
Gawked at your gaudy mortal balloons
Their fingers and eyes hungry for gewgaws.

After the war, you imported thousands
Of plywood fiddles, and sold them
At half-a-crown apiece, to some old fiddler
Who would take them and bury them in shallow
Graves, in the uncertain soil of Dublin gardens
For six months or more, to resurrect them
Like Viking bones, grown mouldy and seasoned
Their ears clogged with gritty earth;
To sell them all summer long
At feises and fleadhs all over the country
And no one could tell them from the real thing.

# Glasnevin Cemetery

With deportment learnt from samurai films
I surface in the ancestral suburbs.
My grandmother is older than China,
Wiser than Confucius.
I pace my stride to hers
Soaking in the grey-green air.

Under my name cut in stone
My grandfather lies
Within hearing of the lorries' roar
Out on the main road.
I forget my unseemly haste
To see the Emperor's tomb.

We search for family graves
In the suburbs of the dead.
From the jumble of worn stones
Unmarked by celtic crosses
Like an Egyptologist she elucidates
Obscure backstreet dynasties.

We see where Parnell lies buried
Under Sisyphean stone
Put there my father says
To keep him from climbing out.
I am surprised by ancient bitterness
Surfacing among the TV programmes.

The plotters of the nation
Are niched in their kitsch necropolis.
Matt Talbot, Larkin, Michael Collins
A holy graven trio
Shoulder to shoulder enshrined
In the tidy bogomil parlour of her heart.

The day flowers sluggishly
From the stone of contradictions.
The trees sway like green hasidim
I shuffle in a lethargic dance
A sprung sign among the signified
A tenant in the suburbs of silence.

From
*Another Nation:*
*New and Selected Poems*
(1996)

# Cigarette Elegy

Nobody smokes like the men of my childhood
with their *Woodbines, Sweet Afton,*
*Player's Navy Cut,* flashing eternally white
and virginal in their stained hands
the dark gold of the tobacco gleaming
in the grime of the morning busses
trundling through the streets. How they inhaled
the metallic smoke, like two gauntlets
hard, black, reaching down into their lungs
to grip like a hammer the heart's worn handle!
They inhaled, with gulps, like men
drinking the wine that had been promised
as if each one was a disaster averted
a moment won back from the devourer of time
their eyes focussed on no point
their sunken cheeks sucked in silence
like a hummingbird swallowing sweetness.
But you, you never exhaled,
no, you held your breath, singing dumb
till your unwritten skin turned yellow
and cracked, and what does it matter
if they inhaled you deep
in the earth's brown lung
or consumed you as you once consumed
in the fire that watches men, cigarettes
and stars go out one by one
to be not reborn?

# The Song Of The Earth: Epitaph For A Dubliner Of The Fifties

Right from the start you were underground
Never sticking your head above the parapet.
Passive resistance, acceptance, survival,
Call it what you like. Your weapons:
Evasion, drink, conformity, laughter. I hesitate
To use the obvious Ostblok/Diaspora metaphors
But they fit. Listening to the babble on the streets
I try to translate you into a grey, truthful voice
But it's not yours. When I write your life's Yiddish
It reads like bad German:
We swallowed our Hebrew a long time ago.

Now you've crossed the river to the third shore.
In the grave you'll speak with a mouthful of earth
You'll stay silent and let them smell the rot of your breath.

# Night In The Suburbs Of Dublin

Kept awake by conscience
And nineteenth century coughs
I try to crash the language barrier,
Soliloquising for hidden cameras.
Someone groans, an everyday ache
Not worth talking about.
I listen, I breathe.
Language is a listening-glass
A lung breathing the earth.
Useless...the susurrating darkness
Ulcerates: a dog howls
Like a god remembering the world
He meant to create
But couldn't find the words for.

# A Protestant Graveyard In County Monaghan

The stone of the church is warm to the touch,
mottled by sodden zephyrs.
The grass lisps a mute stone anthem:
*we lay down on the earth*
*and wrapped its damp plaid round us.*

Inflamed by autumn,
a tree blazes silently
like the flag of the perfect country.

# At The Grave Of Father Hopkins

Outlandish accent in ancestral earth!
The clods drift and turn
through your sightless skies.
You are here, reluctant guest
at the wedding feast of Dublin's dead.

In this hated here, you shed
your unloved body to be married
in the earth with the humble
whose words you plundered
for the still storms of your poems.

Underground, who knows,
they seeped out of your crumbling ears
to rhyme with memories of
Christmas trees on O'Connell Street
and the hidden starlings' tinsel blaze.

Often I bore them, your poems,
past your unsprung presence
but they never called to you
nor you to them. No wonder:
you had gone one remove further

to achieve your final version.

# Words On An Ancient Tomb

Resist! Think how the carved stone
dams your life,
think how tradition begins
with your next word
and be deaf to the vulgarized rant
of the authorized ghost.

Do not resist the day
which turns to stone in your mouth.
You are a bull
who has learned to eat air.
Listen! – how your heart verbs
the waiting dust.

# Glasnevin Cemetery Revisited

The ghosts of machines danced
excruciatingly in their bones.
Coins chipped their hands.

Their bodies lie in the earth
like wet fires, discarded shards
in the potter's field.

Groundlings
in the shadow of words
secreting silence.

The tress *whisht*:
silence veils the rant.
The day sinks to hush.

Flesh is their marble in mortmain.
They left me a free hand
to tremble above their palimpsest.

And yet their blessing wounds;
their pain infects this page:
our alphabets are maculate.

# Afterimages

I looked out the kitchen window
down into the street
and the eyes
of a neighbour woman
being carried on a stretcher
into her house to die.

The women were hoisting you
onto the couch
when our eyes met:
that this could happen
to any mother's son!
That even Groucho Marx
was a member of this club!

Eve's belly
was smooth as a wheatfield,
rope of nothingness
snaking through the eyes.

That night, we played
all the Requiems we had:
Verdi, Brahms, Mozart...
at each record's centre
the navel of death.

I thought of the black whore
I saw in Amsterdam
framed in her allegorical window
shining like polished darkness,
how her Day-Glo purple girdle
gorged the light.

# Death Of A Poet

'Der Tod ist ein Meister aus Deutschland'
*Paul Celan*

Why did I find it so hard to talk to you?
It wasn't just your deafness, or my own
smirking guilt at being at home in this age.
No, it was something more. We disagreed
on nothing of importance, but I hated your life
hated your house arrest in your own survival.
I didn't want to believe your life could happen
because it offered no room for redress
- and I was too Irish to go that naked.
Often, you mentioned the Mayor of Cork,
how as a youth in Haarlem you followed
his hunger strike, his slow descent into victory.
McSw-*ee*-ney or McSw-*eye*-ney, you always asked,
with the attentiveness of the autodidact.
But of course, I never knew. On dark mornings,
descending the stairs in the coffin-narrow house,
I would hear your brisk shuffle in the study
already haunting your own books, and I thought:
it has always been like this. Just once,
at a party, you angular with alcohol
spouting Hölderlin to some German girl,
I glimpsed you as you must have been –
blond, bony adolescent in love with that
language's deadly mirror, those black waves
soon to break in your ears, and your diamond boss's
comic despair, sending you out
to write poems in the café at the corner.
After, you built a house in the dunes

and kept your eyes fixed on the sea
your ears pinned like butterflies.
That curious stance of yours...
shoulders bent, head raised expectant.
Even then, in those '50s photos with your daughters
I see how you were pointed elsewhere. Even then,
you were waiting, with what patience,
with what longing, you were waiting
for the angel to return and kiss your heart to ash.

# Snapshots From Jewish Amsterdam

## 1. *The Wibautstraat*

It's years since this city froze.
The water is soft and stinking,
the tourist boats circle aimlessly.

In the evenings I emerge
from the city's watery maze
like a weevil from a cheese

to stand here near your monument:
a four-lane highway
out to the suburbs

where I too could have been born
in the resurrected '50s
to hopeful parents

in public parks
holding us up like offerings
to shiny new Kodaks

and in the evenings
kicked a ball with Johan Cruyff
down endless concrete summers.

Now I loiter and listen
for the whirr of angel wings
the screech of diamond on diamond.

Nightly, grey water sluices
through my veins while I wait
for the first brittle grin of ice.

## 2. *The poetry and pathos of Social Democratic architecture*

The trick is to make red brick
perform like natural stone, to build
the diamond city that lives in the blood,
that wants to crystallize
in words and acts
but so often settles back
smouldering, like lumps
of half-burnt coal on the landscape.
Fuck Hegel. This is different.
This is the diamond we are born with
or better, the diamond we are
no matter how softly accoutered
the head gnawing itself
in hunger, like a hard flame.

## 3. The diamond workers

An obvious one. Saved,
like the best wine, only till last

they did what they had always done
until, on the day of the last *razzia,*

they stood with their arms in the air
and let the diamonds trickle down

to form a pool of salted light
in which they stood, stranded.

Later, a soldier gathered them up
with a sweeping brush.

## 4. Max Beckmann In Amsterdam, Winter 1944/45

The road from one day to the next
crosses a narrow bridge
across the Amstel river,

takes him through the emptying streets
rehearsing the operas
of the future.

The winter is hungry for men
its swollen sky
and gluttonous light.

Like ambulant mass cards,
the people he passes are ringed
with icy black auras.

At the zoo,
the hippo floats
in the foul water

like the world's sum total
of intransitive verbs.
His mind full of hippo,

Beckmann feasts his brush
on Quappi's thighs and waits
for the squadrons of platitude
to arrive at the City Gates.

## 5. Near the Portuguese Synagogue, Winter 1990/91

Hell has frozen over
and the children skate upon it,
their steel carves the ice
into a jewel of perfect absence.
So let the diamond fall from your hand,
leave it uncut,
a raw fragment of stone in the heart:
let the business-like dusk reveal
a box of left-behind light.

# Dublin 1982

Broken and sad as dusk in an Asian city
an Orientalist landscape
crookedly hung on a concrete wall.

You have half-forgotten your lovers' names.
You married a boor and built a hurdle
your children couldn't jump.

You will not recognise them
prefer to watch your decay in the mirror
a stranger to yourself

a displaced person from wars
fought on your streets, wandering
in the world's washed-up trash.

Your buildings collapse like Berlin
in slow motion: your wall is still intact
and sometimes visible.

Out of your dead meteorite heart
the suburbs are scattered like rubble
a no-man's-land between tenses

barbarians at the gates of Rome
hiding behind the names
of rustic villages.

Your children are all exiles
whether they stay or go:
in your mad microclimate

the heart swears allegiance to nothing
but the palm trees swaying
in freezing rain.

# Dublin 1987/The Salmon

The salmon is what the river sings.
You swim in my blood like a dull crystal.

My blood silvers and deepens.
You grow in my brain like lichen.
You are my concussion.

You are the place
Where thirst is slaked with thirst.

# A Love Song In Ireland, 1988

I'll love you till the end of time
He said, a dark cave opening
At the edge of his words.

The round silver names
Were in his mouth,
The warm mud.

Their sleep is water.
They float together.
Each night his prayer is the same:

Let us dive, let us be propelled
By the thick engine
Of our love,

Let us be the salmon
Who follows a river
Through poisoned seas.

# Dublin 1990/Emigration

This country's half-life
is running out, and still they leave
leaving half-lives behind
to stretch their traces across the globe
to live the life that is left to them
and to know this, always:
we ourselves alone have made the weather
and I myself alone could do no better.

# Ut Pictura Poesis

Our fascinations draw us
– towards what?
Our selves, the truth, to be
repeated and repeated
biological acts?

Maybe they just draw us.
I only know that patrolling galleries
something in me is woken and soothed
by the savage poultice
of Beckmann and Munch

with the velvet crunch
of mirrors mating
a pen bursting
into silence
drowning out the scratch of letters.

But now, out of that blue
nick of ink
on the tongue
a word bubbles into my mouth:
Cumiskey!

Those displaced syllables...
My ear remembers his aura
orphaned among the O's and Macs
blue angel of memory
sharing my bench in drawing class
where I pose in my mind's eye
at the end of that first decade.

See my small black heart!
Sulky Marrano,
making the sign of the cross.

My left hand hung useless
plotting the future
my right hand
aped the ways of men
drawing a landscape I'd never seen:

a white cottage with yellow roof,
stack of turf against the wall
and behind, the Marian skies
the brown pyramid
mountains –

the Free State ikon,
to be executed daily
till its imperfections
were caught to perfection
a prayer repeated till it cursed.

But Cumiskey was different.
Though scooped like us
from Irish muck,
the skies of another Europe
leaked through his hands

till everything he touched
turned the muddy blue
of reality: people, houses,
hills, horses, were all alike
were all like

some Black Theatre, some
shadowgraph smeared
with tears and hunger,
Plato's cave converted
to a bomb shelter.

I looked away from his paper
to the skies beyond the window
smudged, sinister
in that moment
before the lights come on.

They never do. The picture's jammed.
Starlings fall dead
from my nerve ends
and the drying paint
mourns the light.

# The Words

The rusted sword which wields me, say,
is skittering down the rocks of a Wicklow mountain
scattering into a film of light
laving the scree.

Somewhere a seagull shrieks
and lifts itself into the air,
heart's *luftwaffe*,
skirling leitmotiv

of my slow sixteenth summer
when I sat in my room reading *Ulysses*
looking out over the city
to the Sugarloaf mountain.

One dull Sunday I charged up its slopes
*faoi geasa* to reach the summit or die
the earth falling way beneath me
the ocean vaulting up behind

to find when I reached the summit
I had become a cardboard profile of myself.
O static weightless wrestling
to get the light behind me

and shoulder my shadow onto the page
to neither speak nor move
but lie here and not lie
like a dam across the river

and let the flow obliquely tell
the words whose meaning I am
through which I pass
like a slow bullet!

# An Emigrant Ballad

The suburbs of Dublin
are full of roads
which lead to nowhere
breaking off abruptly
in mountains of churned-up mud.
Like unfinished sentences
they say: 'I love – ',
'I hope for –', 'I dream of – '.
Once I thought that all
these roads led somewhere, some –
but it's better not to
give it a name.

This road leads to the airport.
In the departure lounge,
a young man approaches me,
a ticket in his large red hands.
He asks if I know the way
to the plane for London. I do.
'Do you mind if I follow you?' he asks.

And he does, a few yards behind.
Whenever I look over my shoulder,
at the top of the escalator
at the cash register in the duty-free
he's watching me, hesitant, almost
smiling. He sits on the edge of the seat,
and we talk, he's seventeen,
going to his uncle in Croydon:
'But I've got the return, like.'

Last night I dreamt I was back in Dublin
trudging those empty roads again,
my German Army combat jacket
buttoned up against the wind,
fusillades of rain
sweeping the road before me.
Is he still behind me? I don't know
but I can't look back.

# Wolfe Tone

In the dunes at Texel
an old tune raddles the air
but I'm the only one who hears it.

I am becalmed.
The day hangs slack
as a sail without wind.

A shout in the hills,
drums in the narrow streets –
a native land.

And what if I were to find it
and look upon it
*as if it were the coast of Japan?*

# Displacements

*1. The Old Fort In Leiden*

The square root of conquest,
and its surplus. The moon splashes down
on the stone dung of this old fort
where I plant the rhetorical flag of myself
above streets full of blonde aboriginals
their bellies bland with the food
of five continents. Ach,
my patronising *absitomen*
sticks in my apocalyptic craw.
Your infrastructure blinds me
but I'm too half-hearted
to damn or bless, come in
out of the cosy cold
to warm myself at your dead ash.
Evening land...evening land...
a thin German tune shafts the night
and I feel the Gordian knot of twilights
and dawns, rises and falls,
like a black ball in my stomach.
It must have been something I ate.

## 2. Lost In Space

We cycle out into the postwar suburbs
where nothing has ever happened.
I like it here, the milky way of lives
and television sets, crammed
with roads which lead
from nowhere to nowhere –
like one which rears up now
in the suburbs of memory
lit up in the dark afternoon
by a shimmy of tinkers' caravans
cruising like a runway
through the muck
of old potato fields
to end abruptly in detritus.
I played there in the ravaged woods
building fires from debris
warming myself at invisible flames
the wind tormenting their
hot red roaring heart.
I imagined myself the survivor
of some medieval battle
the derelict cars in the ditches
were slaughtered knights.
I was the last man on earth,
or maybe the first.
The rooks scour the skeletal
air of winter, clamourous ikon
sketching itself in charcoal
etching my eyes and ears.
Darkness comes loping
through the trees, like the ghost
of a barefoot gaelic army.

I ran back through the rain
till I hit the concrete
and kept on running, homing
in on five o'clock and my favourite
programme: *Lost In Space*.

## 3. Homage

Home in the concrete igloo, silence
seeps out of the dead TV.
Upstairs, a pageant of dead languages
words deafening each other
till one by one they fell silent
into the long night of the book.
I take down Kuno Meyer, old technologist
of displacements, dusty green parrot
stamped in gold, and read
that great ninth century poem
of the warrior's tryst after death,
how he stands there on the riverbank
and asks: 'What is this place?'
None may address him.
His mind is gapped with purple,
pain blurs his reception
the world comes and goes,
dislocated. And I am found,
my life is here, in this moment's mirror
this capsule shooting through time
with myself, the good doctor,
and the dead warrior, locked together
by a dialectical accident
a twisted crystal which flickers
on the screen of language
a salmon that leaps
from the darkest river.

# Umlaut

*Georg Trakl d.1915*
*Francis Ledwidge d. 1917*

Dreaming at my desk, I've built
this fantasy round Georg Trakl,
which seems to satisfy something,
somewhere. It's partly based
on a tale my mother told me
or maybe something I read
one schoolbagged afternoon
in the Banba Second-hand Bookshop.
It takes place in Navan,
that rivered and mirrored town
on a day in 1917.

Matt McGoona, Meath Chronicler,
heard his friend's boneshaker
rattling into the Square.

He ran to the window, but it was empty.
In Flanders, Francis Ledwidge's bones
shook in the air.

Then a figure appears
on the banks of the Boyne,
between Navan and Slane.
His quicklime head burns the air
his uniform is the colour
of a soiled dove. He sings,
and a passerby hears, in Beauparc,
the blackbird's **umlaut**.

# The Irony Of America

1.
I'm so far from here. Out
of the forest's familiar speakers
an African symphony blares. For days,
we thought we heard the telephone ring,
but no, no one was calling us,
not even that bird. Nor was he calling
the others, on whose lawns and buildings
a siege of flags proclaims:
*we are here.*

2.
New York is peopled from European novels.
Last night we brushed past
a group of red-faced Poles, shirts open
to the cold air. They could have been
my Navan uncles, gilded youth
of an emptying village
off to a dance in 1960, smelling
of drink and soap. On one side
of the street, Perzynski's travel agency,
on the other, a row of funeral parlors
like airport departure gates
sailing East.

3.
We saw him outside the Ukrainian Church,
a blond, bearded, woodcut giant
muttering to himself, lurching
in huge broken shoes his human steps.
He should have been a Holy Fool,
but he's on the wrong planet:
his suit is in shreds, his torso
naked as an unwound mummy. Here,
there is no redemption,
when stumbling, with all
the gravity of America he falls.

4.
In the early years of this century
Samuel Goldwyn, begetter of dreams
lodged in the Rotterdam lodging house
belonging to Abram Tuschinski,
both of them part of a wagon train
scattering West. Tuschinski stayed,
to build a caravanserai
of dreams, still standing,
though he himself, like Perec's mother
was shipped back East to die.
Sam Goldwyn embarked for America:
watching their figures shrink
on the pier, he waved
and shouted: 'Bon Voyage!'

# To A Child In The Womb

Little Brendan, snug in your coracle
you are right to be sailing west
to surrender your tonsured head
to the wave's harsh lick.

Your clerks have copied our manuscripts
in every one of your cells
decorated with birds and beasts
such as you'll see in the New World.

Here in the old country
the Dark Ages are always beginning
and the light that was in Troy
falls on empty motorways.

We are standing on the shore
our feet sinking into the earth.
We raise our hands to bid farewell
to catch you when you fall

over the world's edge.

# Birth Certificate:
# Amsterdam, 22 June 1988

1944: I hate those barbed-wire numbers
evil crystals breaking the light,
death's rusted formula.

Two broken crosses.
The clawprints of a monstrous bird
gouged in a century come to grief.

There is no road. Our bodies
are flimsy bridges
across the unspeakable river,

and out in to
these bloodswept streets
we will carry you, alone.

Yet this year of your birth
has a pleasing shape:
two annealing eights

like the brief eclipse
of bodies when
your flesh was made flesh.

Though I know it solves nothing
though I know
it salves nothing

you have been born.
Saar, I carve your name
on the dawn

and the diamond ratchet
of your small song
turns the wheel another inch.

# Iceland

My pale daughter runs in the wind
which reminds us that this is North.
No patriot could love his fatherland
as she loves this playground
where I hear her shout in a language
I forget in my dreams.

Now, more than ever, she looks
like a child from an Icelandic saga
the foster-child, concubine's daughter
booty of war undeclared
and merely economic.

This January is too cold for tourists.
Like the ghosts of themselves the canal captains
grip the wheels of motionless boats
and Vermeer's 'radiant pigments'
drown behind their diked eyes.

Daughter, I wish you islands
rising like equations
from the ocean of your life
where people rush down to the shore
to gather you into themselves
shrieking in the tongue
you did not believe existed.

# From
## *In This Life*
## (2011)

'In order to write poetry you must first invent a poet who will
write it.'

*Antonio Machado*

# Elegy For A Basset Hound

Other dogs feared you, perhaps rightly –
All that weight so close to the ground
The heft of those padded shoulders
The not-so-comical teeth concealed
Beneath your sadman jowls and pouches.

English-bred and born, according
To the Basset experts, my neighbour plucked
You off the *autostrada* near Lucca
Where you were wandering confidently
Like a nineteenth century English explorer
His mind gone in Antarctic snow.

You settled into an Amsterdam bookshop
Your basket firmly placed between
*The New York Review of Books*
And *Literature in Translation*
Where you accepted the ministrations
Of single gentlemen, but fell in love
With my wife and daughter,
Running away from home as often as you could
To climb like a legless man onto Judith's lap
Where you slept for hours with one eye open.

Untrainable, unbiddable, I could barely hold you
Back on the days I took you with me
To collect Saar from her school, and
You made a beeline through the crush
Of mothers and bicycles, to the class where
The children fought to touch your mighty ears
As you gambolled ponderously on giant paws
Like an Ottoman pasha in his harem.

And yet I loved you for something else:
How on a brown December night
When the light had soaked into the wet ground
I saw you through the dusk of Utrechtsestraat
With trams and teatime traffic crashing between us
Out of earshot, almost out of sight,
You turned on the crowded pavement
And, like the old God of the kabbalah
Lost in the darkness and unknowing before Creation
You raised your nose and sniffed the fouled air
And I knew that you had found me.

# England, Our England

Not the thing itself, but where it is, and where it has been.
Amsterdam in August, and the smell and chill
Of the green canals stalk the afternoon like a ghost.
We stride the Amstelveld like white English heroes –
You, the grandson of an Odessa butcher, whose son
Became a Jungian rabbi, and me,
Whose grandfather wore khaki
In Salonika, in nineteen seventeen.

What could be more apt than for us to play cricket
On concrete flavoured with Amsterdam dog shit?
Your cricket bat of English willow is your most treasured
Possession, a parking meter is our wicket.
You wave your bat, I throw the ball.
Our daughters look up at us with the scepticism of their
    Dutch mothers
But run with us anyway, as if this were some village green
    in Surrey
And not the Amstelveldt, where the coke dealers
And copywriters eye us blankly from the café terrace.

We often translated all night in your red office
Pausing only to surf the cold lawns of the chessboard
And sip single malt, while rehearsing routines
From Tommy Cooper, Hancock and Max Wall.
Outside, the city slowly pulled itself together
And we stopped to make breakfast for our girls
Before they cycled off to school.

We were just passing through,
Translating ourselves from country to country,
To see what, if anything, is not lost
In the Chinese whispering game of the species.

All that is not lost is England, our England
The light growing cold as we chase our shadows
In the Amsterdam twilight
And our daughters' voices mimic us in the dusk:
*'Out! Howzat? Leg before wicket!'*

# Talith

We sleep beneath your grandfather's talith
Fine lamb's wool striped black and white
A giant barcode to be scanned by God
The pelt of a fabulous beast.

Little tent, portable temple
It survived Dutch looters and Dublin landlords
To shelter in this Irish night even me
Uncircumsized, and all too often, unwashed.

Your father pinned it to his study wall
A flag without a shield. Eternity's quilt,
Your grandfather didn't think he'd need it
When he took the train in Amsterdam.

'And what,' he mocked your father,
'Are they going to murder us all?'

# In This Life

*i.m. Katherine Washburn*

I had forgotten you were dead. You stumbled suddenly
into my mind, the way you stuttered out of your taxi
one Christmas, en route from Rome to New York.
I thought you the last of the old New Yorkers
unashamed of what you knew, always ready to learn.
By eight in the morning in our basement kitchen
the ashtray was already full, and the coffee cold in our cups
as we talked of Bukovina and Paul Celan's last poems,
Scholem and the *Origins of the Kabbalah*.

Outside, it was still Ireland.

All that winter, we were like a spacecraft
stranded on an alien planet. Not a hi-tech
Hollywood silver machine, but an old rust bucket
from a low-budget movie. Our cracked capsule
was called 'Seaspray', perched on the rocks of Sandycove,
its eyes watering in the wind from the Kish.
The 'Little Big House' we called it, on account
of all the tiny rooms behind the imposing façade,
and there we waited for the great wave
to lift us off the rocks.

That winter we nearly froze, as I scuttled upstairs
with buckets of fuel, but
nothing could cut the chill of inheritance
from the freezing air, or halt the slow fall
of the damp wallpaper, collapsing under the weight
of a century of servile respectability.

Shivering in our kitchen, you looked like a medieval nun,
or rather, a Beguine, a handmaid of the Lord in her spare time,
with your dusty black dress and your Plymouth Brethren hair
clutching your Mac Powerbook like a latterday missal
crammed with half-done translations from the *Greek Anthology*
and fiery funeral orations by Rabbi Isaac De Fonseca.

Two weeks later you were dead. And we had to leave that house
spinning off into outer space, clinging to debris.
A politician lives in it now, and fills the rooms
with her own air, ignorant of what was buried there.

Katherine: we sat in the Clarence Hotel, drinking vodka
martinis, laughing at how well we knew each other
though in this life we had hardly met.

# Messiah Of Manhattan

The Jewish girls in the library of the Theological Seminary
Have the new-hatched look of nuns, their legs
Are naked and pale and flash like fishes' flanks
When they cross them, perched on high stools
As they scroll through time on their screens,
Pilots of a ship landed here at the top of the island.
Below us the rest of Manhattan steams, limping
Into its posthumous existence, muted, shorn, strangely diminished.

Up here, there is the sound of fountains without water
As the light floods through the huge windows. In the elevator,
A girl with old-fashioned hair smiles at me,
Like a messenger from the future. Surfacing,
I zoom up to the fifth floor, Rare Books Section
To meet the grim Dutch prose of Pastor Thomas Coenen.
With gloved hands, a bad-tempered Russian hands me the book –
One of twenty-six printed in old Amsterdam
In Sixteen Sixty Nine of the Xtian era.
While Pieter Stuyvesant was milking his cows
In the green fields of New Amsterdam, Thomas was herding
Human souls in the New York Babel of Smyrna, where
He saw the False Messiah with his own elected eyes
And wrote a sober account for his masters,
The Dutch East India Trading Company, assuring them
That Time Had Not Yet Ended. They trusted no Messiah
But the hard gold in their purses and the cold storm
In their Churches, not even the wave
Which carries this brittle book to my hand,
Floating above the wrecks of a thousand ships
And half a dozen Temples.

Down at 42nd Street, the shuttle weaves
Back and forth to Grand Central Station
Till its steel wears out or the people have left, the people
Who paint angels on the fire house walls, but
I can tell them, there are no living gods here.
I know the waters will douse the phoenix's ashes
Because down at Ground Zero, we saw the seawall exposed
Holding back the ocean, like the gills of a great fish.

# The Cormorant

'My heart is in the East, but I am in the West.'
*Judah Halevi*

Hard to believe that these were once
an emblem of the soul
these big, creaking machines
whose shit-and-drool fouls
the towpath where I walk.

Like a new tribe in
from the Amazon jungle, they live
on the city's margins,
begging for stale bread.
They have no fear, and without
fear there is no wonder.

On weekends and holidays the immigrants
flock to feed them, taking photos
of their children with the swans,
to send back to Russia, to Lithuania,
from where,

a hundred and fifty years ago,
their neighbours flew out
of a Chagall painting
to end up here
in the redbrick nests of Dublin's
'Little Jerusalem':

half a dozen streets, eleven synagogues, one
for every village in their corner
of that Slavic swamp
where they had built a huge
virtual landing pad
on which the Messiah could land at any moment
like Pope John Paul in the Phoenix Park
descending in his gleaming white chopper...

\*

I rise early on my birthday
to watch the sun on the Wicklow Alps
from this glass room, like the bridge
of a ship moored canal-side.
From the street our friends look up to see us
perform on the family stage.

The swans are there below as usual,
quietly beginning another day's work
when suddenly out of the East
like the Wandering Jew,
comes a cormorant

black as the flag which filled Paul Celan
with such ecstasy
flying above the the barricades
in Paris '68.

Dead centre, a yard above the water
he threads the canal through the city.
The swans ignore him as he passes
through and just above them,
and, without an inch of deviation

flies right under the arch
of Harold's Cross Bridge
dragging my heart with him.

# The Moscow Suburb

I

In all the suburbs of Muscovy, the poets
Are writing their farewells to history,
Hoping to jump the gun.
But history has not forgotten us.

Though it seems to have forgotten
This place, where we walk
On the stumps of gravestones
And the walls of ruins are visible

Under a thin layer of earth,
A city like a lost kingdom
In the Himalayan valleys
Of European memory:

Bastard child of Germany
Sweden's long-lost relation
Estranged suburb of Moscow,
Russian capital of a Latvian nation.

Riga is a place to lie on your back
In a nineteenth-century apartment
And hear the rain tunneling through the drains
While someone upstairs practices Debussy

And feel the delicious clattering
Of stiletto heels on cobblestones
As the girls cross the square with a pink
Flame clenched between their thighs.

II

'It all happened so quickly…'
Said the girl in the Museum of Occupation.
She hadn't laughed when we asked
'Which Occupation?'

'It all happened so quickly…'
Is what her parents had said
When she asked what had happened
To Riga's Jews.

Yes, they saw the lines of men, women,
Children, marching down Moskova Iela
From the Moscow suburb, past the red-brick
Warehouses to the station.

One minute they were there – the architects,
The dentists, the orchestra musicians –
The next day they were gone, and
It all happened so quickly.

III

But still we know what's happening.
The yellow Hummers inch their way
Through the cobbled streets of Riga
Gaudy version of their cousins in Baghdad

Essentially doing the same job.
Nearby a pipeline passes
Carrying gas from East to West
And with it flows of cash and credit.

Like mullet gathered at a sewer pipe
Behind their tinted windows
The Harvard MBAs, technicians of theft
In their handmade Italian boilersuits.

IV

I too marched like an eejit
From Parnell Square to the Dáil
Protesting against the war we knew
Would happen anyway.

I like being able to use that verb: marched
Because that's what people do in History.
But we weren't marching, we
were just hamsters running on a wheel in a cage.

V

Russia is an ocean
Flooding, receding, leaving
Behind pockets and rocky pools.
On Saturday mornings in summer

The Russian wedding parties
Gather to be shyly photographed
In front of the huge granite statue
Of Lenin's Latvian Riflemen

Which the Russians left behind
And the Latvians don't dare destroy.
In white high heels and dresses
Of primary colours I never knew existed

They smile, but hesitantly, as, stateless,
They pose patiently before
The totem of a lost tribe
And wait for History to find them again.

*Riga, August 2006*

# Eight Poems by
# Mikelis Norgelis

Translated from the Latvian by Michael O'Loughlin

# A Latvian Emigrant Bids Farewell
# To His Beloved In Riga

I

Your breasts shine like dark stars
In this black hole
Into which we disappear.

When we are together, you said
It's like we're in a cocoon.
I place my palm on your hot stomach

I feel a strange wingbeat.
You are a white harvest
And I will reap you.

II

You never sleep. All
night you lie beside me
and when I surface,
your eyes in the dark
are like the lights of a ship
anchored offshore.
'What is it,' I say, 'Do you
think the Russians are coming?'
You never answer. Once I woke
to find you cradling me, holding
me tight like your child,
your eyes huge and close to mine.
I smiled, said something, and sank
back down into the forests of light
even then, thinking: I will remember
this at the moment I die.
Now, I think it was the moment I die.

III

Late arrivals, we fly in the dark
the airport is already full in the European day.

Just after dawn,
you told me you had imagined all week
that we were both dead.
You saw it all, the hospital wards
the graveyards, some kind of *liebestod.*
I told you what it meant,
and then we slept, or almost slept
our fingers laced together like a zip
our palms like locomotive buffers pressing
and then we dreamt, or almost dreamt
that we were high above the city, walking in light
outside of time, until we were woken by the urge
to tell each other the same thing we had dreamt.

'Now I know we are one,' you said,
between sleep and dream.
But you are wrong. I will be flying
through the European night without you, alone
in the beer-drinking crowd.
I will close my eyes
but time will not stop
because time, like love, will always fuck us.

IV

Keep dancing, Princess
on the Square in the Old City.
It is night, the snow has stopped falling
you are dancing alone
to music only you can hear.

I am travelling West
to bury my heart in an Irish bog.

# A Latvian Poet Writes An Ode To Capitalism

It was all very well for Pablo Neruda,
Mayakovsky and all those comrades
To write their Odes to Labour: they had
Stakhanovite steelworkers,
Drivers of red tractors breaking virgin soil.
But what about me? How am I to praise
The call centre operative,
The barista in the boutique hotel,
The estate agent renting out boxes to Slovaks?

I sit here eight hours a day in my blue uniform
At the cash register in Tesco's
Trying to think of a name
For what I actually do.
My co-workers are called Mariska or Muhummad
I do not know where they live
I do not know what they eat.

All I know is we are low-caste priests
In the greatest church that history has ever seen.
The people come to the altar rail,
We lay our hands on the fruits of the earth
And give them back to the people who made them
Blessed, sanctified, paid for.

No, I don't feel up to writing an ode to people like myself.
Anyway, there's a party in a flat in Baggot Street
And the guy from Brazil has some really good dope.

# A Latvian Poet Does The Joycean Piligrimage

A cynical priest shows me the room
With the pink and white stucco ceiling
Of Diana the Huntress
Where you once knelt and prayed
And dreamt of Monto whores.
Leaving, I pulled open the big front door
Precisely as described in *The Portrait*
Facing down the long black valley
Of North Great Georges Street.

I descend it, as you must often have done
Into Dantean Dublin, past the blue light
Of the Cobalt Café, the pavements
Lined with Lithuanian cars.
On the hostel steps, men are standing
Smoking and speaking Russian.

At the corner of the street
Named after your uncrowned King,
Filled with call shops and Chinese restaurants
I buy five bottles of Latvian beer
In a shop called Booze2Go.
Special offer: Five for Ten Euro!

# A Latvian Poet Encounters
# Róisín Dubh

I

You make me rub your back till the skin is red and broken
you make me press your bones till they crack.
I want to reach my fist down
deep inside your chest
to pull out your heart,  and hold
it up to glisten in the light
hard and black as a piece of bog oak.

I want to fillet out your spine
and have it mounted in Kildare Street
alongside the Great Irish Elk
just to make the poor extinct fucker quake.

II

I like it when you sleep
and I press my nose against your skin
you smell of rain on the hillside
you smell of nothingness
you smell like a Neapolitan saint
emerging from her coffin
after a hundred years in paradise.

III

You lodged beneath my skin
like a sliver of glass. Good pain
when I pressed, it made me feel alive.

Now you move like the Minotaur
through my body's dark maze
to carve me like an invisible butcher.

IV

The Vikings would have loved you,
would have chased you across the peaty hills
your white feet splashing in black water
and torn you like a kitten from Mother Ireland's paps
from which you drank your poison straight.

They would have known who you were
but embraced you anyway, as I do
believing all men are lucky or doomed,
and taken you back to your sister, Gudrun,
who goaded four good men to their death:

Thorkel the chief, Bolli the comely
Thord the wise, and Thorvald.
Grown a pious old woman, she'd say:
'The one I loved the most
was the one I treated worst.'

# A Latvian Poet Reads Yeats' *A Vision*
# In The Oliver St John Gogarty

Ireland is such a wet country.
Beer and vomit, semen and piss.
In the downstairs toilet an English woman
Is having sex with two Irish men.
Up here in the kitchen the Chinese giggle
And the Polish porters glower.
Me, I'm starting my coffee break
So I can return to Yeats' *A Vision*
I like to smoke and read a few lines
And let his words roll round my head.

Strange to think that all of us –
The Poles, the Chinese and me –
Once were children in shining white shirts
With little red scarves around our necks
Singing songs of Hope and Progress
Not  knowing we were the Beast
They feared so much over here
That we almost blotted out the light.

But the Beast is dead and
We have come crawling like vermin
Out of its cold fur.

Now my break is over,
And it's back to work. I
Have to bring down some beer,
Huge barrels like steel pills
To be forced down the throat of the serpent
Which fills the streets of Temple Bar.

There is no longer any darkness in the world.
The light shines in every corner.
I cannot sleep, I cannot dream,
Like a medieval Latvian serf I wait
For something to wait for.

# A Latvian Poet Spends Xmas In Foley Street

The streets are strangely full.
The neighbouring families swell
With new members. What's going on?

Outside the all-night Spar
A girl pushes her tongue in my mouth
Like a hungry fish.

'I'm out of the 'Joy for Christmas,'
She says. 'Can you tell me
The price of a packet of fags?'

# A Latvian Poet Listens To Irish Songs

What they do to us, these songs
The ballads of Transylvanian Gypsies
Tangos, fados, Georgian laments –
The music speaks to us in words
We cannot understand, except for one or two
Stepping stones which lead us over
A river of black emotion.

Like these Irish songs I hear in pubs
Or on the local radio. Some words
I have learned to recognise,
Like *muir* for the sea. That's an easy one,
Cognate with Romance languages.
Then there's *croí*, for heart. That's harder
But still not far from *coeur* and *corazon*.
But what about words like *brón* and *uaigneas*?
And my favourite, the word for red: *dearg*
Strange and contingent as our Latvian *sarkans*…

Do I need to learn this language to understand
The songs? No.
Sea and heart, sorrow and red,
The story is always the same.

Like that girl who works in the corner shop
Where I buy my cigarettes.
I don't know her name or nation
But her eyes are a country which invites
Me to explore its hinterland.
Every day we talk until

I stop and she stops, and she smiles
And waits on the threshold
While I look into those bogholes, thinking:
At the centre of every eye
A circle of blackness, the same
In every woman I've ever loved
And then I say goodbye and turn away.

# A Latvian Poet Climbs Killiney Hill

This city has dyed her hair blonde
And had her breasts remodelled
To look like the whore
In the hotel foyer
Anywhere in the world.

I want to know what she looked like before
So I climbed Queen Victoria's Hill
To look at the famine obelisk
Because I know that hunger
Is the true God of the Irish.
It came down from the mountain
And gave them two commandments:
Thou shalt devour and thou shalt hate
And laugh and dance and sing to fool
The angel of death into thinking you're alive.

Looking down the hill at the muddy path
I think I see her looking up, half-crawling
Yellow maize porridge cakes her lips
Her breasts hang slack and luscious
As dying fruit on her ribcage
Which trembles like a songbird's throat.

Her skin is white as the mushrooms
In the cold ground of the Latvian forest
But her eyes and hair are black
Black as the wind in the thorn bush
Black as potatoes rotting forever
Deep in the black earth.

# The Widows' Prayers

'Origin is the goal.'
*Karl Kraus, quoted by Walter Benjamin in Theses on
the Philosophy of History*

You were born to be a widow. Not that you
Didn't love Michael O'Loughlin,
My father's poor father,
But you broke him anyway
The way you broke your five strong sons.
I've read Freud, I've read Jung
But there's nothing here to analyse:
Their theories break on your brute existence
Like snow on a bonfire,

Leaving you intact,
Proletarian bitch goddess
Virgin Queen patrolling your realm
For thirty years, obscenely alive
Moving amoeba-like
Through these ancient streets
A monument to mere survival,
Life at its most stripped down.

Your widowhood was electric.
I remember my uncles, giants
Kneeling at your feet
In the tiny kitchen
Of the house Big Jim Larkin gave you
Smaller than the cars they had parked outside.
You shrank them like some sci-fi machine,
Even now the perspective dizzies me
The only thing that was constant
Was the framed photo of Michael Collins.

All your life you played
In the giant Las Vegas
Of the Catholic Church,
With its Casinos of Sorrowful Murmurs
And their one-armed bandits of the soul
The flashing lights, the bells
The jackpots of Lourdes and Fatima.
I'd love to know what deal you struck
With the thing you claimed created you.

In my *Wanderjahre* I wrote to no one,
Friends or family, trying
To pare myself down to essence
But in every town I came to
I hunted out the local Virgin, always surprised
To find there was one, and sent you postcards
Of her different faces. We never
Talked about it
But you placed them in line
Stuck in the frame of a picture of the Sacred Heart,
Beside the Child of Prague, in your front bedroom.

Why were you the way you were?
Original Sin or Oliver Cromwell,
The Act of Union Eighteen O One,
Twelve to a room in the Georgian tenements
The impacted pain, the squalor
Of drunken soldiers rollicking
In the biggest brothel in Europe,
The strikes, the Lockout, the Somme,
The black and tan shot dead
In the local fish and chip shop,
The Free State army who shelled your house
With borrowed British armoury?

In that holiday snap from the Twenties
My blond blue-eyed grandfather,
Home from the war in Kerry
Shirt-sleeved and smiling
Lies relaxed on the Free State beach
Having survived a second time.
But you are sitting upright beside him
Dressed in your Sunday best
Bristling with black energy,
A backstreet Sphinx on the sands
Your face insolent, ignorant, unreconciled.

You loved me more than you did the others –
Maybe you saw something of yourself in me
Maybe you put something of yourself in me.
What was looking out at me through your
Transparent blue eyes but the species,
Nature, and Mutation, Chance and Necessity –
The O'Loughlins are a family of gamblers
But I never did.
Maybe I myself am the gamble
Rocketing round the map
Like a roulette ball, unable to choose
Between red and black, aware
That the house always wins.

Now I take the new electric tram
Through your native realm, and
I pass through those old places: the church
Where you had me initiated
Into the rites of your tribe,
My first school, the distillery
Where you took me to one day
To meet my father, emerging
From this brick and copper cathedral
Of noise and sweet smells
Wearing blue overalls and a mask
Like a figure in a Socialist Realist painting.

And as I look out I always think
Of Polanski's film *The Pianist*
Where the tram bisects
The Warsaw Ghetto
Filled with people not staring
At a zoo whose business
Was survival, and now
Like this one has disappeared
Beneath designer restaurants,
Shining apartment blocks.

I'm beginning to understand why I keep
Sniffing round ghettoes, in Amsterdam,
Riga and Wilno, looking for my childhood
Streets, now gone like Ruthenia, a country
Which only lasted for three days.
Three days or a thousand years,
What does it matter
To Benjamin's Angel Of History
His wings propelling him to Paradise
Gazing backward
At the growing pile of debris?

His focus tilts the planet and time
Like a child's kaleidoscope.
Decades and distances blur
From Volgagrad to Dusseldorf
From Dublin to Barcelona
He sees tens of millions
Of old women, walking painfully to market
With string bags and coloured headscarves
Struggling against the wind,
The wind that is blowing him to Paradise
And looking back he sees
The air singing with the dead
And how the widows' prayers come together
A cloud of grey radioactive dust
To enshroud the fading planet.

# A Stone For Queen Maeve's Tomb

It was the kind of funeral you'd want to avoid –
The unwed bride thrust into the ground
Dressed in her unworn wedding gown
While the bridegroom tottered at the graveside

Peering down dizzily at his future life.
He flung the rings down after,
Eternity devoured by time, and her
Teenage nieces shrieked like bewildered beasts.

A cloud doused the sun and the hole
Was a tunnel sucking us down, but
The open grave gagged on us, so
Bitter was the taste of life

Its black teeth broke on our indissoluble earth.
And then the day was huge and blue
And streaked with veins of light
Like death's lucent afterbirth.

Here, Maeve, a stone for your cairn
Eimear O'Driscoll of Rosses Point
From Deutschland and Dublin returned:
Here she was buried, here she was born.

# The Muse

'Break on through to the other side…'
*The Doors*

Lord: this is too difficult
To worm my way into a shroud of flesh
To feel my mouth fill with red life
That tastes of death
Like a blunt hammer-headed shark
Drawn convulsively to its own bleeding wound.

Devoured, devouring, I break my head
Against the dark walls seeping light
And always I am left like this
Weightless and heavy as water.

But today,  I broke on through to the other side
And found what I did not expect:  You,

An Italian widow,
Waiting alone on the cold, sunlit piazza
Drinking coffee black as your eyes.

# The New Cemetery

The first implants in this bleak field
which slopes down to the Tolka river
are slowly being cemented
into a new suburb.
Even as I write, your future
neighbours are moving house
borne aloft on morphine biers
or rudely pushed through screens
of steel and glass. No matter.
Their new homes wait.

But for now, the only other grave's a local gangster –
he died, famously, in a taximan's lap.
Still just a kid, he'd killed
too often to be let live.
His grave is now adorned with toy cars
and trinkets, footballs, an empty
bottle of Jack Daniels…
And on the marble carved the usual tributes:
'Wonderful son, beloved brother.'
I am none of these things.

# Parnell Street

'Death will come and will have your eyes.'
*Cesare Pavese*

This is my first address: this is where
My mouth first opened. After half a century
I'm here again, as if the Rotunda midwife
Had never cut the cord.

Fair shades, my first loves
Stand at the Finglas bus stops
Or shelter in  the doorways of  extinct pubs.
Here is the basement where young poets
Cuffed each other with sheathed claws,
The attics where we rehearsed our lives
As *Songs* by Leonard Cohen.

In the surprisingly beautiful Fifties flats
Behind the Georgian façades
I returned to film children
Who saw religious statues move –
The old gods' last performance.
Now the gods have gone
But those children's children
Still play on the streets
Fearless and insolent as ever.

The world has followed me back here
Like multicoloured gum on my shoe:
Now I hear again every language I ever heard
Drink beer I crossed a continent to taste.

The old Shakespeare Pub is a Korean restaurant
But nothing has changed. Men and women
Still face each other at tables, trying
To rewrite the night to a different ending.

In dreams I often returned here, looking
For my life, which was hiding
In an alley like a wounded animal.

Now I am afraid that
This is where death will find me,
Wearing your eyes.

*New Poems*

# The Traveller Girls At The Siberian Ballet

The Travellers have settled. They have settled for this,
the last stop on their itinerary.
They have been so long walking, but now
the songlines are silent
from Ballinasloe to Ballybane...

From my room, I see their houses
boarded up like faces...

\*


Siberian swans have flown from Perm to Galway
to perch and dangle on the Town Hall stage.
Skinny, frilled, and blonde they streak the air
in this dark town,
as Tchaikovsky is squeezed through the speakers
distorted and distant but still
delivering big pink thumps to the heart.

Leaving the theatre,
the pure faces of the Traveller girls
glow with illumination, like the Buddha as a child
not quite smiling, but watching in bliss
like an astronaut orbiting Earth in his capsule,
gazing on the planet they came from and will return to.

Their teacher tells me: 'They're fine
till they hit puberty, then they just disappear.'
To where? Into the karmic wheel
of birth and death and suffering, where time
makes them settle, so they stand still
for the rest of their lives, camped
between avatars, stunned
by the shock of unmoving ground beneath their feet.
Only for weddings and funerals,
fiestas of eternity, time and traffic stops.

In the evening I see their fathers' impenetrable faces
as they speed their vans from one end of the car park
to the other, and back again and again,
the children strapped into their cots
to let them dream before they fall
and wake to see the ground
rushing up to meet them,
making them halt.

# Dublin 1812

Shelley slithered like sperm
up the river, into
the cold womb of the city.
A cold womb for freedom –
it washed you out
in the grey bidet of the Irish Sea.

Cloud-botherer, crowd-baiter,
you were a white mouse
dropped in a nest of vipers.
(But shure, there's no snakes here
your honour, Sir Percy Bysse,
Baronet-to-be of Castle Goring.)

You would free the haberdasher!
Make the chimney sweep your equal
and the coachman your brother.
You didn't know the ancient Irish triad:
liberty, equality, fraternity –
three things we do not want.

# Psychopomp

*i.m. Mary Tierney*

On your deathbed you joked:
'remember the time I nearly died?'
but Mary,
you have gone down into a place
blacker than your wit

Your body dreamed of its own decay
wet leaves, rotting crab claws,
the queasy downward spiral
into material

'Mathematics for ladies!'
I always made you laugh
with Joyce's quip about Bach –
you were a Zen maths teacher:
on their first day you took
your convent girls to crochet class
to show them how mathematics
is just God knitting the universe...

We are not things but theorems
of which the proof is death.
Our last day on the South Wall
you frantically took photos
of the light on the water
the pink, the blue
the mountains reflected above and below
as if trying to prove a thesis:
how could all this beauty vanish?

But it does.
And we are just fading photos,
dancing pixels spinning
to a halt like a wind-up toy
leaving a hole in the light

And if I say I'll see you again
it's knowing
there will be no I, no you
and nothing will be seen

# The Black Heralds

after Vallejo

There are hard knocks in life, I don't know,
knocks as hard as the hatred of God, and faced with them
the hangover of everything suffered
wells up in the soul, I don't know.

Few and far between to be sure, but they dig
dark ditches in the fiercest face, the strongest back.
Perhaps they are the steeds of barbarous Attilas
or the black heralds which death sends us.

They are the fallen depths of the soul's Christs
of some adorable faith blasphemed by destiny.
These bloody knocks are the crackling
of bread which burns on us at the oven door.

And man, the poor unfortunate! He turns his eyes
like when summoned by a hand on the shoulder,
he turns his maddened eyes, and all he has lived through
floods, like a pool of guilt, into the gaze...

There are hard knocks in life – I don't know!

# The Literary Life

In my room on the top floor
There are no blankets, so I sleep,
Like a Russian poet,
Beneath my sheepskin coat.
As in a child's angry fantasy, I eat
What I like for every meal: bread and cheese
And cold beer from exotic bottles.
On the table, the only other furniture,
Is my typewriter, an *Erika* made in the DDR
And biographies of Berryman and Lowell
Which I am reading in stereo,
Once again taking a cautionary tale
For a user's manual (I made
The same mistake with Joyce and Ellman).
I'm trying to write a poem about them,
Going for a kind of jaunty doggerel:
'*You poor old sods*
*You thought you were gods*
*Or the nearest thing to it:*
*Greatest Living American Poet...*'
The final lines will have something to do
With the 'Your move, Cal' note anecdote.
It's not working. Down four flights
Of coffin-defying stairs
The streets of Amsterdam are full of muses
But I need to sleep. I lie down
And watch from my bed
The solemnly, blackly dust-jacketed Haffenden
With its iconic portrait (maybe in McDaid's?)
And the fatter, yellow-covered Hamilton
(American edition), with its thick luxurious paper,

A gas-guzzling Cadillac of a book.
All this, I think, will someday
Be like that, as I fall asleep
Eyeing the tomb-like volumes,
Carefully trying to avoid seeing
The few scattered sheets of paper
The white overhelming
The tentative ants' column
Which tomorrow will march on
When, unlike Berryman
I will wake regenerate.

# The Getaway

For years I loitered outside
used car lots, picking
the vehicle I'd use for my getaway.
I was drawn to an old brown Mercedes
the kind of car you could drive all night
to Donegal, to abandon on the strand
and walk away from, eyebleached
and empty, watching the sea.

I was called to the hospital
because you'd gone missing.
'Clever man, your father,'
said the Filipino nurse.
'He put on his clothes beneath
the blankets, when the shift
is changed he ask to go to toilet.'
You ripped out the plastic tubes
and then you just kept going,
down with the lift, through the foyer,
ducking and diving across the carpark
and out into your childhood streets.

I'm with you old man,
in the back of that taxi,
the drugs dwindling in your veins
the blood seeping down your sleeves,
as you speed down the motorway
making a break,
heading for the hills,

your Roman nose cleaving the air
like a Legion's standard.

# Conleth O'Connor (1947-1993)

You came into the Grapevine Arts Centre
like a ghost from someone else's past.
We nosed about you like young horses,
veteran of the small press wars.

I dubbed you 'The Polish Playwright'
for your beard and flat black hat,
buff-coloured duffel coat tightly strapped
around your fading pinstripes.

A bookkeeper ruined by books
auditor of your own epitaphs,
you sat before work in the office carpark
drafting poems in your old *Volks*.

Grim golfer, manic strategist,
cranky, obnoxious, irascible,
and me the smarmy young bastard, all
Saul Bellow to your Delmore Schwartz.

I followed you, a surly apprentice
as you pushed through the drinkers
in suburban lounge bars
your belly wielded like a meaty fist.

A self-taught *samizdat* modernist,
but there was more, something ancient
something spavined, something, for want
of a better word, Irish.

Yet distant Europe was your element.
Or, as I put it in my prissy eulogy:
'He grafts an imported technology
onto a native temperament.'

Prophet of boom and bust, I feel
your presence with us again, a revenant
haunting the halted development,
the half-empty shopping malls.

We sat in your room on Widow's Row,
'what I laughingly call my library',
your face a rictus of hatred and glee
as you handed me a review

In which *The Irish Times* wrote:
'Why is this on the national radio?
Who is this man we don't know
telling us things we don't care about?'

# A Hospital In Amsterdam

In her blood the black and white knights
clash – the black is silent. But the white
hums all night in the darkened room, a soft
robotic whisper pumping life back into her
attending her bed like an X-rayed angel,
the antibiotics digging in
like the Red Army at Stalingrad, to cross the river
and swarm across the landscapes of her brain.

Morning explodes like mortars
with Amsterdam's everyday pulse:
piledrivers sinking their sting into sand.
Flip this city over,
you'd be looking at a petrified forest,
each pile driven home
by the huge hydraulic Singer
stitching us into the earth

like me sitting here,
trying to sew back on Vincent's ear.

# Acknowledgements

*Poems 1980–2015* includes poems from the following books: *Stalingrad: The Street Dictionary* (Raven Arts Press, 1980*)*, *Atlantic Blues* (Raven Arts Press, 1982), *The Diary Of A Silence* (Raven Arts Press, 1985), *Another Nation: New and Selected Poems*, (New Island/Arc, 1996), *In This Life* (New Island, 2011).

The new poems in this volume originally appeared in the following publications: *The Irish Times*, *The Stinging Fly*, *Southword*, *The Stony Thursday Book*, *Cimarron Review* and *Berryman's Fate: A Centenary Celebration in Verse*, edited by Philip Coleman.

Special thanks to the Centre Culturel Irlandais, Paris, and the Patrick and Katherine Kavanagh Foundation.